Dr. Andrey M

HARNESS THE POWER OF CONNECTION

ACCLAIM FOR *HARNESS THE POWER OF CONNECTION*

"Andrey Gidaspov has done a masterful job of redefining the art of fundraising into a message of positive collaborative change. 'Fundraising is a part of philanthropy—loving the agenda of humankind.' He tells his readers, 'You've got to be thinking 24/7 about other people—not just what they can do for you, but what you can do for them,' and his focus on interconnectedness has the power to vanquish the ill-ease committed fundraisers have all felt at some time about the simple act of asking for money. Cold knocking on doors, 'begging' for funding—even for great and important causes—can be painful at times. But as Andrey Gidaspov so skillfully lays out in his book, the real message is that it isn't about money at all—'it is the chance to give others joy.' Filled with pragmatic, practical hints and tips, this is an upbeat must-read for mission-focused fundraisers with a need to engage 'knowledgeable and passionate people in a meaningful way.'"

— Patricia Bader-Johnston, CEO, Silverbirch Associates KK

"In this engaging, easy-to-read book, Andrey combines humor and approachability with key advice, insights, practical examples and creative ways of doing things. Oftentimes, I have observed a short-sighted approach to fundraising, meaning transaction-like relationships and short-term gains at the potential sacrifice of long-term, sustainable relationships and results. The key differentiator of this book is that it offers a lens to fundraising with a long-term strategic outlook, one that will bring enduring results, ensuring that there is a more sustainable pathway for your organization's program or cause."

—Wameek Noor, former Director, United Nations Foundation

"As a director of a 501c3 nonprofit, I found Andrey Gidaspov's book both inspiring and practical. In this book, Andrey explains why you shouldn't give credence to wild dreams of asking Jeff Bezos for money, but rather look to practical steps to get your fundraising kick-started. Key to this is understanding that fundraising 'is a chance to give others joy' and delivers an 'intangible emotional boost' to donors. Nonetheless, Andrey makes it clear that action is one of the most

important aspects of your fundraising, along with building and nurturing relationships with donors."
—Nicholas A. Kosar, Director, Associates of Colonel Philip Ludwell, III, Inc.

"This book is great gift for small non-profits! As the founder of a small international organization, I rarely have a free minute. And when I find time, I try to spend it productively, learning new things that can benefit my non-profit. Andrey's fundraising book is very practical and informative, and I can use his advice right away. If you're struggling to find funding for your non-profit, get this book right away."
—Bobby Smith, Founder, Hope for Lives Sierra Leone

"I found this book delightful, informative, and tenacious. Andrey has certainly taken his lessons learned through work and life experiences and set forth a good guide to fundraising."
—Tyrena Holley, Former Senior Commercial Counselor, US Embassy Ghana

"This book is perfect for people like me who "hate" fundraising and don't feel like they can be successful at it. It breaks down fundraising into manageable steps and offers thought-provoking activities to help get you started. I don't have a strong background in fundraising and it is something our organization struggles with, but this book provides useful tools and tips which we can actually put into practice at the International Functional Fitness Federation. It will definitely take us some time to get things implemented, but I plan to try to use the advice from the book to solidify a better fundraising plan for our organization!"

—Gretchen Kittelberger, President, International Functional Fitness Federation

"An authentic, clear and insightful approach that has proven to be successful. I recommend this book to individuals and non-profits looking for sure answers to their fundraising challenges."

—Andrew Benson Greene, Jr., Founder, B-Gifted Foundation

"Andrey Gidaspov's book *Harness the Power of Connection* is a quick, easy and engaging read that should be part of every fundraiser's library and should be read especially when you have a new boss coming into the organization or when you're not sure why you're doing what you're doing. It's a great reminder why we're in this world as fundraisers and how to really make a difference. Using the power of connection doesn't have to take a lot of time, just some dedicated effort to follow the simple steps Andrey outlines in this book. Every chapter has some quick exercises that will help you get closer to your goal of raising more money for the organization you care about."

—Erica Waasdorp, President, A Direct Solution, author of *Monthly Giving, The Sleeping Giant, The Monthly Donor Road Map* and many other monthly giving resources

"This book is the most practical fundraising book on Earth! It's easy to read, the stories are relatable, and there are exercises provided at the end of each chapter. It's very practical. Smart!"

—Greg Warner, CEO and Founder, MarketSmart, author of *Engagement Fundraising*

HARNESS THE POWER OF CONNECTION

Harness the Power of Connection: Raise Your First Million, Fast!

.

Dr. Andrey N. Gidaspov

Gidastar Publishing

© **Andrey Gidaspov 2019**

ISBN: 978-0-578-48229-3

Cartoon illustrations by Andrey Gidaspov

This publication is designed to provide accurate and authoritative information in regard to the subject matter covered. It is sold with the understanding that the publisher is not engaged in rendering legal or other professional services.

Dr. Andrey N. Gidaspov

Dedicated to Michelle, Alexey, Victor, and Anna

HARNESS THE POWER OF CONNECTION

Dr. Andrey N. Gidaspov

Table of Contents

Why This Book

Whether you're new at fundraising, or have been working at it for a while, this book is an invitation to look at your fundraising challenge through a new prism—always looking for opportunities to build long-lasting relationships with your existing and new partners, sharing your values and making a deliberate ask.

I learned it through my experience as a frontline fundraiser. When it comes down to it, fundraising isn't actually about money. In fact, it shouldn't be. It's about people. It's about shared values. It's about the mutual benefit of changing the world.

Without people who share your values about positively changing the world, there's no way your organization can be sustainable! As such, the core task of any successful fundraiser is to build long-lasting bridges with people who share your values and want to change the world in alliance with you.

When you are equipped with these principles, fundraising becomes a philanthropic endeavor, and your job becomes your lifestyle. You've got to be thinking 24/7 about other people—not just what they can do for you, but what you can do for them, which will lead to a whole web of interconnectedness that will eventually, in some strange and yet unknowable way, come back to you. As such, this book is for those who care about their cause. It's especially for you if:

- you're passionate to change the world, but hate to beg for money;
- you run a small non-profit and have no support staff or even volunteers, and don't have the slightest idea how to fundraise;
- you're a development officer in a small non-profit with limited or no prior experience in fundraising;
- you're a volunteer working your butt off to try to help your Executive Director to find resources for your non-profit organization;
- you're an association manager trying to convince your member organizations to look at fundraising seriously.

Then, please join me in my personal journey on the path of fundraising learning and success. In this book, I will:

- share some specific tips of how you and your non-profit can make your fundraising outreach successful;

- share some examples of how NOT to do your fundraising;
- motivate you on your way to this rewarding but sometimes stressful job;
- ask you to work with me and use the pointers and advice right away, one at a time.

Being a business book junkie, I have always benefited from picking the brains of top experts. Even a small piece of advice given at the right moment can propel you forward. It's worked for me, and I'm sure that it will work for you.

There's just one simple ground rule— you must use the advice right away. That's the trick.

So, if you are reading this trying to decide whether you want to invest in sharing your time with me, I say, "Do it only if you promise to act on it." Otherwise, put it down, and grab a magazine instead. Easy to read. Easy to toss.

Ready? . . . Let's do it!

Why Me? My Journey to Fundraising (or, love comes easy with non-profits . . .)

On our long flight when I was returning to visit our family in Washington, DC, I still could recall the succulent aromas of Hong Kong's bustling Soho district where little cafes offered a variety of fantastic Asian dishes in a spectacular atmosphere that combined a rich blend of Hong Kong history and Chinese and British culture . . . Oh, how I loved being in that city, breathing the air of constant movement, never-ending business excitement, and addictive, innovative ideas! I ran a small, but rewarding, consulting business that allowed me to meet and work with top technology companies in Asia and all over the world. In those four years, I traveled around South Asia, China, and Africa—helping my clients, writing a book, and presenting at conferences.

But at the same time, we were thinking that perhaps we needed to start a new chapter—we had two children and Hong Kong was not an inexpensive place to live. Most importantly, the kids needed more space and we needed to look beyond Asia. I enjoyed having my own business, but I was also thinking that I could be doing more to help the community and, especially, the younger generation.

My chance came quickly. I saw a random advertisement for an international program manager position at a large DC nonprofit combining everything I could dream of—working with China and the other BRIC countries on trade and humanitarian projects, recruiting and mentoring some of the top students in the G-20 countries, helping to make the world a better place . . . This was the change I'd been subconsciously looking for – and I decided to go for it. Little did I know that I was beginning a whole new career in the non-profit sector, and it has been a blast! Everyone in the organization is a fundraiser, right? While I started as a program manager mentoring students and doing curriculum work, I quickly found myself drawn into fundraising. Somehow, everyone else seemed to avoid it, but I saw it as a new challenge.

My first ask came suddenly and with less than twenty-four hours of planning. It was a whim, really. Fundraising is a humbling experience: every time you receive money, you glance into the depth of human capacity to give. On one of my business trips, where I went to South Korea recruiting students for DC-based internship programs, I had one of those breathtaking moments of witnessing humanity at its best. It started with a relaxing morning. While I was enjoying my breakfast at the hotel, I noticed an article about a prominent American lawyer highly regarded in the community for his knowledge and respect for Korean culture, as well as a number of philanthropic causes that he supported. I challenged myself to cold call the office and meet this remarkable person. I thought that this could be an opportunity for us to begin a new relationship. After several calls and conversations with his secretary I made my way for a thirty-minute audience with someone who didn't know of my existence the day before. This was also my last business day in Seoul.

What do I have to lose if I meet someone passionate about education and share what our nonprofit does? After twenty minutes of pleasant conversation, there was only one thing left to do. Ask. I asked him to help two underprivileged Korean students experience a transformational internship program in DC. My counterpart didn't say much. I waited, holding my breath. Silence. He said that he would send us a check shortly. It felt great! Wow, I can do that!

So that's how I became an accidental fundraiser. Not long afterward, my full jump into one-hundred-percent fundraising happened also by serendipitous chance. As I was visiting one of my interns at his work site, I had a chance to speak with a Development Director and enjoyed our conversation immensely. He mentioned that he'd be moving on, and talked me into applying for his position. In his words, "I think you'd be perfect for this role—you have a knack for fundraising." Hmmm . . . all I'd been doing, actually, was building relationships and connecting people, just like in every other job.

So, I landed my first "real" fundraising job. I found myself facing so many needs, all at once, with so much seemingly undone—possibly, what you're facing now. I needed to launch a new development strategy, work with volunteers, figure out my Board members (who I could count on, who couldn't I?), and, of course, find new funding sources. With time, I did all of that and more, just as you will, too. And over the past decade, I've supported several other non-profit organizations, each with its own challenges and opportunities. This included working with various Board members who had already firmly crossed out the organization on their lists for monetary support, and then reviving their interest again; pulling off hugely successful events on a short notice; and doing two major campaigns at once, just because a new boss thought that nothing's impossible! I've tried to pull many lessons learned from this trial-by-fire in the pages which follow.

4

As I went along, I knew there were plenty of similarities with other jobs I'd had. For someone with a business background, there is an element of a sales process, like creating a sales funnel and building a lead pipeline, but there was something very special and different about this. I needed to "sell" the vision of my mission yet had no tangible product or service to offer in return. What surprised me the most was this: it didn't matter! Donors were happy to give, because they were actually receiving something: an intangible emotional boost—a feeling of having made the world just a little bit better. And that in turn gave me a similar boost. We, as fundraisers, are changing the world, one donation at a time! What an amazing feeling!

I also learned quickly that there are plenty of naysayers—those folks in the organization who say we've tried that, and did this, and none of it worked. I'm sure you hear those voices, too. So, this makes your job of relationship-building so much more important—both inside and outside your organization. Your best tools are empathy, listening, and an incessant search for opportunities—and, with these, you'll gradually build wins to quiet down the naysayers.

In reality, fundraising outreach was really similar to traditional business development and sales. As I fine-tuned my way to apply these principles to prospect-building and donor outreach, it became really rewarding. More than anyone, I was more willing to go after those big fish and make bold requests. What's the worst they can say, right?

Getting a nod for my first million-dollar check was satisfying. In fact, it was amazing! No one in my organization at the time understood how I'd done that—they didn't know about the hours I'd spent on the phone with the donor, listening genuinely and building our relationship. This work is quiet and simple and behind-the-scenes. However, if I were to distill my strategy in simple terms, here are the most important pieces of my fundraiser equation:

See: You must be constantly looking for opportunities. Your job is to become a scanner of possibilities, someone who consciously seeks promising leads and valuable connections. Be like a bee who is flying around the meadows collecting the nectar of the future. BUT you always should start in your own backyard. That is where the flowers are nectar-proven!

Connect: Connecting requires deliberate preparations and thoughtful execution. Connecting is the art of making separate dots a part of one core. Connecting comes as a lightning bolt that jolts your counterpart with energy to make things together. I invite you to think of connecting as the chance to showcase what you can do for others and how you can share your values to benefit both sides.

Share: Only by sharing your values and sharing your willingness to help your partner organization can you establish a truly synergetic relationship. Share your time, share your experience, share your efforts, and you will see how productive your partnership becomes!

Act: Well, I've seen plenty of fundraisers who prefer to sit in the office and juggle email, participate in office conversations, and create plans, plans, plans . . . without really doing anything. However, we are all perfectly aware that only action breeds success. A successful fundraiser is always thinking about reaching out with the ask. There are two tools in your pocket: ask for advice and ask for money. You don't need a third one. These two will perfectly deliver every single time.

Treasure: It's extremely important to treasure your relationships. And don't get me wrong . . . when working with donors and partners, you shouldn't be the one who spams and annoys your counterparts with untimely messages pushing your services. Instead, you should be very thoughtful in your stewardship process, helping your donors see bigger rewards by digging deeper within the wealth of offering.

To develop these habits, it takes a combination of patience, deliberate practice, and, yes, an element of luck. Yet the rewards are simply immense! Let me share with you how it can be done so you may sense the exciting realm of the possible. This has been a great ride!

Andrey's Little Truths

Take things in stride: When your plan is not working as you'd hoped, breathe deeply, and spend some time at a local coffee shop to think it all over. Reflect on your experience, and when you do, you'll be able to put things in perspective. Are you there to make quick wins? No, you are there for the mission you believe in. The rough patches will pass, and in the meantime, these folks need you!

Use the professional skills you already have: No matter what you were doing before fundraising, you learned something about how to work with people. Use that insight—use everything you already have—to benefit your fundraising project. You don't need to reinvent yourself for this job.

Look on the bright side: No matter how dire things look, there is always a bright side. Having an optimistic outlook inspires your team and helps you reach ambitious goals with less effort. Yes, some of us were lucky to be born with a smile on our faces, but anyone can apply the positive thinking process! It will help move mountains.

Trust your instincts: I can't repeat this enough! Don't be fooled by the naysayers; you can find those people everywhere. If you know deep inside that something is going to work, then go for it. Despite, despite, despite the naysayers! I've been in many non-profits that were governed by skeptics with a painful attitude of "been there, done that!" That's soul-crushing for your staff to hear, and most importantly, dims your results if you let it.

Nothing happens until you act: It might sound obvious, but I've seen it again and again: consultants, partners, board members, and the whole gang keep talking about goals, about new ways of doing business, about new tweaks, for months or more, and nobody moves ahead. What you need to do in fundraising is to be constantly moving, and nothing, repeat NOTHING, should stop you from acting on your plans. Even if it's just one phone call, make sure you reach out and engage every single day. That's the true key to success!

Your Relationship with Fundraising (or, please don't use that "F" word again)

Before we get started, let's first talk about your own relationship with fundraising. How do you feel about it, really? The first thing I learned about fundraising in the non-profit sector was that ninety-nine percent of non-profit staff members strongly dislike it! I would often hear in staff meetings, conversations around the water cooler, even Board meetings:

- "I HATE fundraising!"
- "I don't even want to think about begging!"
- "I'm an accomplished scientist—I despise the fact that I have to go and ask for money! I work for a science association, not a sales club!"
- "Please do me a favor—don't mention the "F" word!"

There are so many similar phrases that I've heard throughout my career. Have you heard these, too? Do you ever feel this way?

I remember how in one of our staff meetings, a tight-lipped, well-respected staff member cringed when she heard another call to support our fundraising effort and could not hold her composure any longer. She railed at me: "I loathe this word, and don't you count on me for anything on this. I joined the non-profit sector because I care for education and I want to help communities—not for this!" Bummer! I'd always respected her, and continue to, but this really made me feel sad.

The good news is that you don't need to continue these scripted conversations, because fundraising shouldn't be a curse. You need to be ready for these conversations, for sure, but first you need to be convinced yourself, and be firm in your heart about what fundraising is. Fundraising should bring joy and excitement to both parties, the donor and the asker. In the words of Hank Rosso, fundraising gives others the opportunity to experience the joy of giving! Joy, happiness, a rewarding experience—not hatred, begging, or embarrassment! Fundraising is a part of philanthropy—loving the agenda of humankind.

So, when you walk into that staff meeting, remember:

- Fundraising is not a desperate plea for money—you are not a BEGGAR;
- It is not a half-baked ad-hoc decision to get some QUICK money;
- It is not "We tried it and it didn't work, so why should we do it again?"

- It is not "Let's plug in our interns and volunteers and send them to fill in and make the ask at the event."

Rather, it is the chance to give others joy. It happens when knowledgeable and passionate people engage in a meaningful way with others about their mission. These are substantive conversations, not desperate pleas. And it's your responsibility and your opportunity to move your organization forward. Think about it this way: Why do you work for a non-profit organization? Naturally: to help your community, to use your best skills to change the status quo, or to use your professional experience to help younger people appreciate your profession. Whatever your reasoning, you can't reach your ambitious goals without the extra resources that only fundraising can help reach!

Exercise:

Can you share what fundraising means to you?

Let's think about why you're doing this in the first place. Write down below the reasons you want to help your non-profit grow. What are your dreams for your organization? What could you do if you had a limitless amount of funds?

_____

_____

_____

_____

_____

_____

Now, finally, think about those cynics in your meetings. Take a minute to reflect for a moment on what objections your most outspoken naysayer might raise, and how you could respond. You can jot your notes here if you'd like.

_____

_____

_____

_____

_____

Some Ideas to Consider:

At many of the non-profits I worked with, I organized a special meeting under the rubric "Everyone IS a Fundraiser!" And here's how:

- Book a conference room. Use a flip chart or white board and write: "What does Fundraising mean to you?" Or: "What is Fundraising?"
- Invite all staff members to share their perspective on fundraising. Give them five to seven minutes. They can write their answers on sticky notes and stick them to the board.
- Read out a few answers, and begin to reflect and interact with participants.
- Share the perspective that donors actually get joy from the opportunity to donate.
- Give them a primer on the ABCs of Fundraising and the Fundraising Cycle (Prospect – Cultivate – Ask – Steward). Discuss and explain each part.
- Discuss ideas on what each of the staff members can do to raise the bar at your organization.
- Incorporate both your and their fundraising outreach ideas into the conversation.
- Get a call for volunteers.

- Offer "an open-door policy" to help staff members and volunteers with their fundraising questions.

Dr. Andrey N. Gidaspov

Part 1: See & Connect

HARNESS THE POWER OF CONNECTION

Bill Gates or Warren Buffett? Look in Your Own Backyard First

I'm sure that you've heard the following phrases a number of times, as I have: "I have a fantastic idea—let's reach out to Bill Gates (Warren Buffett, Jeff Bezos, Mark Cuban, or fill in the blank . . .) because they just gave out a billion dollars to _____!!" Wouldn't it be super easy to do? Think of it, these billionaires have gobs of money, and surely, they want to know better what is going on with our non-profit!

Don't fall for this trap. Yes, I encourage you to try this outreach, if there is a connection with your organization. But you should not live on wishful thinking. Yes, this idea sounds like a cool option to those who don't want to build a sustainable fundraising system that will help your organization for many years to come. But if you analyze how many non-profits have already been seeking the support of these star individuals, then you probably would skip this call. (On

19

the other hand, if you have someone on your board or a volunteer who can give you a warm introduction to these folks, that makes it a totally different game.)

Instead, look first in your own backyard for prospects! When was the last time you had a deep, meaningful conversation with your top donors, or a long-term Board member, or a well-connected community volunteer? If you haven't found the time due to your busy schedule (and small non-profits are always busy with a gazillion things to do!), do it first thing after you read this. You know why? Because it can lead you to something incredibly fulfilling. At one of the non-profits that I worked with, there was a great group of dedicated Board members who, unfortunately, had become less and less active in fundraising due to various plausible reasons—they had been helping a number of other non-profits, were tied up with family obligations, or simply had lost an active interest in the organization.

When I joined, I wasn't intimately familiar with the industry, but I knew how to work with a Board. Let me say it now, and I'm sure you'll hear it again from me: the Board is one of your most important assets—don't underestimate this resource! So, I decided to plan for some quality time with each Board member and made sure that I traveled and met with all of them one-on-one in order to give complete attention to each of them. I wanted to show how important they were for the organization, and how valuable their advice was to all of us. I planned each trip thoroughly, to make sure that I carved out some quality time with each. I also prepared a brief (and sincere) plea to them—that I couldn't do it without their support! Remember that all these members are humans and they can quickly decipher if something that you say is genuine or a bunch of fake statements.

The result was simply unbelievable. After I'd built this rapport over several months with individual members, I raised the issue of the lead gift at one of the Board meetings, and said that I'd be following up with each to ask how he or she could help. To my delight, one of the individuals who'd been with the organization for many years called me and asked me to visit him in his office. Little did I know that after just a twenty-minute conversation, this very generous and kind-hearted gentleman would gift us with a seven-figure contribution! Think of it—is it worth it to have a deep conversation with your Board members this month? When you do it, DON'T ask for money right away. (We'll talk about timing more in the chapter on asking.) Instead, as you build your relationships:

- Be Genuine.
- Be Inquisitive.
- Be Respectful.
- Be Curious.
- Be Authentic.
- Be Your Best Self.

Exercise:

Here is your homework for this week. Go ahead and knock out #1 and #2 today!

1. Print out a list of your Board members.
2. Analyze your past interactions with them.
3. Have you met them all in person? If not, note those you haven't met as high-priority.
4. When is the last time you had a meaningful conversation with them? If it's been more than six months since you've met with any of them, note these names as high-priority.
5. Research the giving history of each.
6. Learn everything you can about each Board member and his or her family.
7. Schedule time on your calendar to do nothing but contact them to schedule appointments. Make sure that you plan for at least an hour-long conversation with each person.

In your meetings, be conscious of how much you're speaking versus how much you're listening. Be engaging and respectful . . . and listen well.

After each meeting, WRITE DOWN your notes.

After each meeting, on the same or next day, take five to ten minutes to write a thank-you note. If you do it right away, you'll find it's a joy and not a task. You'll probably still feel the energy from your connection with this other person.

Schedule regular "touch-base" meetings or calls with them. Put tickler notes on your calendar for these, and act on them!

Mine for a Gem in Your Non-Profit's History

How often do you pay attention to the history of your non-profit? If you joined a non-profit which has a rich history, dedicate at least one day to researching that history. You can do so internally, by checking the data in your CRM and meeting with former Board members and volunteers. You might also do so with the help of the local library. You never know what kind of gems you may discover!

At one of the large non-profits I joined, I was given an extensive look at its past by a knowledgeable and dedicated volunteer. This was one amazing volunteer that any organization would be eager to have! Grey-haired and elegant, well-spoken, and most importantly, super-passionate, he was a treasure chest of the most intimate information about the non-profit. He was so eloquent and knowledgeable about the rich history of this organization that I was truly impressed and taken by his invigorating support of it. Not only he was happy to share all he could about past donors, their history, and miniscule details about the development of this organization, he was also actively interested in helping out in any way he could, as well as ready to learn all he could to support my efforts.

Well, that produced an incredible result! One thing happened during that conversation. He mentioned a piece of information that I thought was amazing, but that he just thought was a simple fact of history.

Listen to what I heard: "During the early 1950s, John D. Rockefeller served as President of this organization!" *What? John D. Rockefeller?!* If I could rewind that tape I would. Of course, I interrupted my friendly volunteer: "What did you just say? Is that true?"

"Oh, yes," he said. "Here's the photo from the archive."

"Wow," I replied. "This is amazing. Has anyone been in touch with the Rockefeller family?"

"Oh, why should we bother them? They probably wouldn't ever return our call. They don't have business with our organization anymore."

(Sounds like a familiar refrain, right? It won't work, so why bother?)

I got right on this one—a famous millionaire right in our own history! A household name! I immediately started my research to figure out who from the immediate descendants might welcome this connection. And after I found my prospects, I jumped into my favorite tool, LinkedIn, and immediately found the right way to connect—through a thoughtful InMail request.

How do you go about it?

First of all, you need to do thorough research and learn all you can about the person's prior engagement and connection to the organization, so that you sound professional. You need to dig up contact information. Once you have that contact information, you need to pave your way to an appointment. It is absolutely crucial to get that face-to-face connection. Figure out who would be the best person to have at the meeting. Who could make a personal connection—the development team, the Executive Director, or one of your Board members?

Luckily for me, I found Justin Rockefeller, the grandson of John D., on LinkedIn. He's had his own career as a social entrepreneur and change-maker. He graciously responded to my message and, after a few calls, we found an opportunity to meet each other in Chicago at a conference where he was speaking. After a few thoughtful conversations, we were able to host him and his brother at our organization to engage them in a conversation on how we could work together on new community projects.

Lastly, remember that with celebrities, having their name associated with a project is often more valuable than any financial donation.

Exercise:

Here is your homework:

Who are the people with the longest history with your organization? Meet with them and ask about the past. What made the headlines years ago about your mission? Who was involved? Ask for photos or newspaper articles. Ask them who else you should talk to—who may have been involved during a particularly intense period for your organization.

Take a trip to your local library and ask for help researching previous projects. You could even do a historical focus piece in your organization's newsletter, and solicit old photos and stories in advance.

If you find some interesting nuggets, do the legwork of tracking down current relatives and contact information. As always, do the work to get the appointment, and use that opportunity to build the relationship.

Connect with Connectors

Okay, we started in our own backyard. Check. But what about if you're somewhere completely new? What if you need to raise funds for your nonprofit where you don't know anyone and have no idea where to start?

I've been there. And here's what I did.

I was given a huge challenge—to revive the struggling fundraising process to renovate a historic building in an old, proud East Coast town. It was the kind of city with not only a quaint, old red-brick downtown, but also a hip, modern edge. Honestly, once I got there, I loved it. The challenge was that I didn't know anyone there.

If you don't know anyone in town, fundraising might be a problem! What do you do in this situation?

Well, you start with what you have. And I had the name of one elderly gentleman that everyone at headquarters said was displeased with the organization—I was told not to get my hopes up. I took a deep breath and gave him a call. He was surprised but agreed to meet me. Our meeting lasted three hours! I listened to his life story, as well as the entire history of his involvement with the organization. He'd been disappointed with some of the decisions that'd been made in the last few years. It turns out he loved our mission—but his passion had turned into frustration. However, with this conversation, it was clear he didn't want to see the organization wither. Eventually he became our biggest donor.

But he did something more important that day: he gave me a slip of paper with a woman's name on it, and said offhandedly that I should call her.

I did, of course. At first, I heard quite an earful. She, too, was unhappy with how things had been run lately. She said she wouldn't meet with me—or anyone else— but she kept talking. I got a word in edgewise and said, "Please—how about just breakfast? I promise I won't ask for anything more!"

That was the best breakfast I'd ever had. This wonderful woman knew everyone in the city! After we got past her frustration, and then into her own story and her family, her face lit up. She saw that what I was doing would help her city, and she got out her phone. "Who do you want to talk to?" The first call she made was to one of the most respected businessmen of the city, who agreed to meet with me, and whose name eventually opened every door in the city for this project. We built an advisory group almost right from their phone lists! This was, you see, a small town, and a passionate one at that. We renovated and reopened that building, and won a lot of friends along the way.

Any place can be a small town if you tap into the right network. You need to find the connectors—the people who know everyone else, and win them over to your mission.

Exercise:

Here are a few pointers for you on what you can do right away to advance your cause:

Ask around. Who knows everyone else in your town, or in your mission area? It doesn't matter if they know anything about your organization. Come up with at least five possible names. Can you do more?

_____

_____

_____

_____

_____

Who in your organization might know that person, or know someone who knows that person? Work through these connections to try to get a meeting, even a short one, with that superconnector.

_____

_____

_____

_____

_____

_____

Spend quality time with this person. Invite him or her for a meeting to listen to his or her advice and brainstorm possible ways to advance your cause. Ask who might be interested in your mission. Remember, don't ask for money—that person's connections and introductions are worth much more.

Important: What local projects might you want to volunteer for? Not only will you lend your time to an important cause, but you will also be able to meet some really cool individuals who, in turn, will introduce you to other people, who will introduce you to other people . . .

_____

_____

_____

_____

Networking with Purpose

Networking has a bad name, but it's all about people and relationships. Before you can have a relationship, you need to meet the person, right? And there's so much potential in the people we haven't met yet! This section includes some nuts and bolts about how to network. The big idea here is that you never know when a new connection will come in handy, so meet and build relationships with as many people as possible!

When you need new prospects, you can't just rely on Google search and email marketing, you need to put your shoes on and go out there—to the wild, wild world of networking. I've been often asked (especially by introverted development officers): "How do you cope with putting yourself out there? How do you get in the door to meet presidents, CEOs of top companies, or celebrities, in order to accomplish your goals? What is the secret of finding your way into their closely guarded worlds? How do you make your business meetings memorable and purposeful?"

If you ask people who know me professionally whether they consider me an extrovert or an introvert, they would probably say, "Oh, Andrey loves networking—of course, he's an extrovert—he loves to socialize! He's all around the room at any event!" The truth is that I am a deep introvert, who happens to have jobs which favor extroverts. I definitely can program myself to work hard in a networking or "asking" environment, and succeed there, but at the end of the day, I will need several hours to chill at Barnes and Nobles or a local library—my favorite places!—to get back to my normal self. So, the point is, even if you don't consider yourself a natural networker, you can learn to get in there and do it. I hope the next few pages make it seem less daunting.

Here is the secret, and it is rather simple: **you need to be networking with purpose.** Frankly, there are no magic tricks, other than to be prepared, be genuine, and be ready to help instantly and follow up.

Let's be honest; most of us are guilty of stalking strangers who seem to have potential as donors, and then when we finally talk to them, we suddenly burst out with a long, long story about our organization's achievements and our personal successes. Somehow, it's always about us. And it's always: "Give me!" Our messages and elevator speeches are often filled with egos the size of the universe. No wonder that the meetings are superficial and results are minimal. But it doesn't have to be this way. Let's remember that the single-best advantage of meeting another human being is to learn about him or her. We should constantly remind ourselves that everyone appreciates sharing his or her own story.

Whenever you're meeting someone new, forget about fundraising and ask yourself, "How can I help the person in front of me, right now? How can my professional or personal connections, or a particular skill that I have, help this person or his organization succeed?"

If you think this way, you might find you actually start to enjoy networking—and you'll find that you're meeting your fundraising goals faster.

For example, I have always tried to file away information and categorize my contacts and projects— to be able to match them with the next person who might need my help.

Here are my five secrets to great networking with purpose:

1. Tune into your contacts' interests: always think of your counterpart's benefits first. Whenever you're meeting a new contact, whether it's a potential donor, business owner, non-profit manager, or entrepreneur, learn as much as you can about his or her trade and specialty.

Understand where the greatest need is and try to fill it. Without a doubt, if you are a "natural giver," in Adam Grant's terms, then it will work easier for you. Here is what this best-selling author of *Give and Take*[1] reveals on achieving success by giving. Grant believes that "being a giver doesn't require extraordinary acts of sacrifice. It just involves a focus on acting in the interests of others, such as by giving help, providing mentoring, sharing credit, or making connections for others." Based on his extensive research, Grant also notes that the main distinction between givers and takers is that their giving "spreads and cascades." Interestingly, people who receive from the givers get excited and spread the same giving spirit, creating a ripple effect![2]

2.   Find out how your skills and connections can help this person right now. Each of us has a unique network of business contacts, family connections, and friends. It's not necessarily all business. Sometimes your counterpart might

---

[1] http://www.giveandtake.com/Home/Index
[2] https://fs.blog/2014/10/adam-grant-give-and-take perfect-elevator-pitch.html

need some trivial help in finding an experienced freelancer, admin assistant, or doctor. Once you figure out that you know someone who can be of assistance, you will need to go out of your way and offer what you can to help him or her. And the point is to ask nothing in return. Just show your best philanthropic self! Most importantly, don't postpone this request—think on your feet and try to help in the moment. Trust me; this will go a long way.

3. Create and practice your elevator speech to perfection. Do you know what differentiates you and your organization from the competition? Can you recite your elevator pitch—a concise description of your company—in your sleep? Next time, before you go to your next networking reception, polish your elevator speech to perfection. YouTube offers plenty of resources to help you with this. I personally like two video lessons on creating your perfect elevator pitch: one by Michael Hyatt, best-selling *New York Times* author,[3] and one by Chris Westfall, the national elevator pitch champion, and the author

---

[3] https://www.youtube.com/watch?v=-t1ar_IpmUU

of *The New Elevator Pitch*.[4] The key points that both Michael and Chris are making are:

- Be clear and concise about your product or service;
- Describe the problem or challenge you are trying to solve;
- Focus on your proposed solution;
- State the key benefit of this solution.

Once you've mastered these points in one succulent elevator pitch, here is what Avi Loren Fox, the millennial founder and designer of Wild Mantle, who took part in the Shark Tank, recommends as the next steps:

- Discover your personal formula, using your personality in your pitch;
- Memorize your pitch;
- Practice somewhere noisy;
- Use a power pose;
- Work with adrenaline.[5]

---

[4] https://www.youtube.com/watch?v=GqsWKaR9Q6M
[5] https: //www.inc.com/peter-economy/5-secrets-for-crafting-the-perfect-elevator-pitch.html

Find whatever works for you, and practice it to perfection, so that it flows naturally the next time you see someone who might match your description of a good lead. You will actually feel good about yourself and see results soon.

4.   Follow up. Follow up. Follow up. (And with a handwritten note, please). People make the mistake of not getting in touch with their newly-built connections, losing the momentum and all the benefits of immediate follow-up. It's amazing how many opportunities and investments of time and effort are lost when you wait weeks to follow up. You suddenly come across that business card and ask yourself in despair: "How do I know this guy?" Whenever possible, try to write a short note about your counterpart's focus on the back side of his or her business card. When you're back in the office, take a nice thank-you card and write a handwritten message to your new connection.

5.   Make an effort to become a sustainable connection. Very often time and our busy schedules take their toll on our business communication, especially when we've achieved

our business goals, and we don't feel the pressure of keeping up with our contacts any more. Naturally, some of your contacts will have more long-term value than others— the thing is, you can't figure out which ones until it's too late. So, make a habit of sustaining all of your contacts—as much as you can—and building this into your daily routine. How exactly can you make your connection sustainable? Try to figure out the ways that you can help your counterpart in the future. You could send her an interesting link or an article, or invite him for a coffee or lunch to catch up on the news. Building trusting business relationships takes time, but it's certainly worth it.

Exercise:

Create and practice your elevator speech to perfection this week! Remember the four keys for a great pitch? Start filling out this information right away. Then practice. (Joining Toast Masters International or the National Speaker's Association might help!)

1. What is your product or service?

   _____

2. Describe the problem or challenge you or your organization is trying to solve.

   _____

3. Focus on your proposed solution.

   _____

4. State the key benefit of this solution.

   _____

5. Check what you learned about your 5 new prospects.

   _____

When you are going to your next prospect meeting, make sure that you record all pertinent information about your prospect in your organization's database:
- Interest in your cause:

   _____

- Support to other non-profit organizations:
  _____

- Hobbies:
  _____

- Other interests:
  _____

How can your skills and connections help this person right now?

On following up:

Check your log from last week's meetings. Do you see any meetings that were promising, or did your prospect request some feedback? Do you recall writing a note (perhaps, a mental note?) to send this person a handwritten note right away when you're back in the office? How about you do it now? Write down the names of 5 contacts (prospects, or current donors) who you might want to write an encouraging note, or a response to their inquiry.

Become a Sustainable Connection

Make a list of your top 30 contacts, and think how you can help your business partners in the next two to four weeks. Let's get your first 5 contacts down right now.

Write their names and the action that you can do to benefit their business:

1. _____
2. _____
3. _____
4. _____
5. _____

*Hint: For example, you could send them some useful links to an article from their field or of general interest. My favorites are from HBR, Inc., FastCompany, or Entrepreneur.

Expanding Your Network with Corporate Donors

If you are a small non-profit with a volunteer board of retired teachers and academics, reaching out to corporations might seem daunting to you, but guess what?

There are real people who work there! People are people, no matter where they are—and you need to connect with them in the same way you do with individuals you see as potential individual donors.

How do you get a corporate sponsorship these days? What are the best ways to ensure corporate support? Whom do you contact to receive funding? What are the most effective ways to reach out?

In my experience with working on getting corporate support, the best way remains the same as it used to be in the past—personal connections.

"Robin, bad news! Our 990 shows – we're down on corporate sponsorships!"

The more you get yourself known to your corporate friends, the greater your chances of success. You need to go out of your way to share the story of your non-profit with the corporations that traditionally support the same issues that you are so passionate about.

The stakes are high. Based on research by IEG[6], in North America alone, corporate sponsorship reached an

---

[6] http://www.sponsorship.com/IEG/files/f3/f3cfac41-2983-49be-8df6-3546345e27de.pdf

estimated $24.2 billion in 2018! That is certainly a nice round figure you could use for your non-profit!

In order to claim your portion of that amount, you need to realize that corporations are profit-driven, and they build relationships on a very pragmatic level. Most of all, corporations want to showcase their genuine care for the community where they operate, which allows them to differentiate their brand and attract more customers.

You need to think from their perspective. Their donations have to be able to boost their image and be visible. So, they will sponsor programs, sponsor events, or name buildings. Rarely will they give blanket funding to an organization.

Does this mean that it is impossible to convince a great corporation to support your cause? Not at all. Let's discuss key steps to making that happen:

1. Thoroughly Research Your Corporate Prospects.

    To be successful in landing your first corporate sponsorship, you will need to start from the most important part—doing your initial research. It's simple nowadays, isn't it? Google your favorite corporation, check out their annual report and/or Corporate Social Responsibility

(CSR) report. Find out who their key officers are. You may need to look at the Board structure as well. Ideally, you want to identify who from your organization might have a warm connection with your target corporation. And you should look at some key managers, like the CEO, Executive Director, Board members, followed by Directors of CSR and Marketing. Usually the budget for funding non-profits is found in either the CSR or Marketing Departments. Corporations work with their community peers through these windows. In my experience, these are two most important departments that you need to focus on.

2. Check out the CSR Report and Community Marketing Materials.

Look carefully at the CSR report and the marketing materials—is there alignment with your goals? The CSR should give a clear picture of the values of the corporation, and the goals it's trying to pursue with its philanthropic work. It's strange, but I've noticed that many nonprofits aggressively pursue corporations when there isn't a remote fit in terms of the values or goals of both organizations.

3. Discuss Your Findings with Your Executive
    Team and Come up with a Strategy.

    Once you've finished your research, and
identified some key individuals, it's time to sit
together with the Board and Executive team to
figure out the right strategy. Think what
programs and initiatives would be most exciting
for a target corporation to support. For example,
not all events are the same, and a potential
corporate event sponsor would have different
outcomes in mind. A company that's looking to
be viewed as a responsible stakeholder in the
community would want to sponsor a major,
public event with a lot of press coverage. On the
other hand, a small, private event with local
political leaders in attendance might be seen as
a more effective event by other companies. Your
options can range from a large gala to asking one
of your Board members to simply open the doors
of her house to host a small gathering.
    Or if you're hoping a corporation will sponsor
a program, consider how you could make it more
attractive to them. They might not want to
sponsor exactly what you're already doing (and

seeking funding for)—you may need to create something new to attract them. For example, you might offer to replicate a successful program in a city where they have a major presence. Or a company might want to sponsor a new award or youth program if it wants to boost its credibility with a specific demographic group or attract future talent. Again, try to view things from their perspective, and get creative!

4. Make it Happen: It's Time to Act!

Well, after you've done your research, you need to test it with reality. Most of all, when you meet with the potential corporate sponsor, you need to listen – just like with any other potential donor. They may have refined their goals, or might be looking for a very particular project this year. Listen, and adapt your offerings to meet their interests.

With solid research, a warm introduction, and a flexible approach, you're likely to succeed. Lastly, if your organization is so small or new that, truly, no one knows anyone, here is a really great way to make connections with top-level corporate contacts—at conferences! Yes, you need to go to the conferences where top-level corporate managers participate as speakers. Your only mission there is to get to these sessions where they are speaking, and "come and get 'em" right after their speech. The fact is that most of the audience will silently disappear, but you'll be first in line with your business card.

Exercise:

Create a list of all past corporate supporters to your non-profit. See what connections you can find between these accounts and your Board, executive management, or volunteers. Make a chart something like this:

Organization's Name: _____

Contact Name: _____

Past Contributions ($): _____

Project Supported: _____

Connector's Name: _____

Develop an action plan to reach out to these corporate contacts:

Discuss engagement with Contact (*Name*) with Connector (*Name*) by Date: _____
Reach out to Contact (Name) by Date: _____
Record a summary of your conversation in your CRM. Follow up accordingly.

Foundation Outreach: Striking Gold (or, "let's do another grant proposal!")

Foundations can be a useful source of funding, but they remain a mystery to a lot of non-profits. According to the Center for Effective Philanthropy research,[7] forty-eight percent of charity leaders say foundations are oblivious to their needs.

If you are one of the tens of thousands of nonprofits seeking foundation grants, you must understand one simple truth: if you'd like to be considered, you need to spend time researching and actively communicating with your target foundation. The same basic approach works with foundations as everywhere else—build relations with the people who work there.

---

[7] https://www.philanthropy.com/article/Grant-Makers-Are-Blind-to/154409

Let me be clear: hiring a professional grant writer and shooting dozens of proposals a year to various foundations will not work. The harsh reality is that foundations are flooded with proposals, and even if you

have a worthwhile project that is going to eradicate poverty, it may not even get to the right person to be considered.

Here is my advice to get results. Spend money or time thoroughly researching your target foundation. If you have a budget for your development department, then you may want to think of buying access to foundation databases. There are plenty of good databases on the market. I personally found FoundationSearch[8] (FS) quite useful. It includes "more than 120,000 foundations, and tools to locate grants by type, value, year, recipient, donor and historical giving trends." What is great about FS is that you'll have your very own account manager who will guide you and help you along the way. Using FS's database, we were able to target foundations very narrowly, and as a result, raised $30,000 funding from a private foundation for a pilot educational program. While the access costs around $3,000 per year, that investment for us paid off ten times!

If you have no extra budget to purchase fancy databases, go to the Foundation Center, [9] and invest some quality time in selecting the right target group.

You could use its Foundation Directory Online which offers a free search tool—FDO Quick Start—providing free, public access to essential information about over 100,000 foundations and over 250,000 IRS Forms 990-PF. You will find funder profiles which include address and contact information, fields of interest, program areas, and fiscal information.

---

[8] http://www.foundationsearch.com/about/index.aspx
[9] www.foundationcenter.org

In addition, you can benefit from various free and paid training sessions scheduled throughout the year.

Once you've done your research, forget about email, and instead, pick up the phone and make some calls. This is the best way to understand the foundation's focus and needs and have a productive conversation with someone who will give you the right answers—and on top of this, appreciate your outreach. You will be surprised how many small family foundations do not even have a website! Granted, you may run into some dry wells along the way, but trust me, you will find some oases on your journey.

And as Amy Eisenstein, ACFRE, one of the country's leading fundraising consultants suggests, you need to make at least two more calls to make sure that you have established a strong connection. The second call after you apply for the grant, "is a good time to ask when decisions will be made and when you might expect to hear. You may also invite the program officer to visit your organization and/or take him or her on a tour of your program or facility."[10]

Use strategic networking to connect with decision makers. Find out about major conferences or workshops in your area where top foundation officers will be

---

[10] https://www.amyeisenstein.com/win-more-grants/

present. Use LinkedIn and foundation websites to learn as much as you can about these foundations and participating staff. Then all you have to do is to prepare your thoughtful questions and have your elevator speech handy. Have you created and practiced your elevator pitch?

Foundations are amazing resources to get your non-profit a much-needed funding boost, but I am still surprised as to how many non-profits place all their hopes in one basket. It is fascinating that many of them absolutely neglect their individual giving programs— assuming that their existing foundation grant will be renewed year after year. The same goes for reliance on government funding. There are so many examples of failing nonprofits who depended too much on their grants, however large they were.

No doubt, foundations provide a great source of funding, but my suggestion to you is to have them as a supplemental resource. In my own mental equation, the time and effort that you need to use to receive funding breaks down as follows:

- Individual (major) donors – 70%
- Corporations – 20%
- Foundations – 10%

That said, here are my final tips on how you can most effectively approach foundations:

- Hire an experienced grant writer or consultant. This will increase your chances for success.
- If you can't afford a consultant, learn as much as you can about each and every foundation you are applying to. This will save you from many needless applications.
- Use facilitators—as often as you can—like FoundationSearch, which I mentioned above. (And I honestly don't own any stake in their company!). I was able to raise tens of thousands of dollars just by using this incredible source.
- Call and meet Program Officers as often as you can. You can gain pointed and great information that might result in hundreds of saved hours.

Exercise:

1. Start with the Foundation Center research. Make a list of fifty foundations that supported projects similar to yours in the past 3-5 years.

2. Record their contact information and responsible officers. Reach out to at least 10 foundations a week to learn more about their funding cycles and requirements for grant submissions.

3. Record your findings in your database, and follow up with promising leads!

Maximize Your Engagement with Multipliers and Partner Organizations

"Friends should be friends," sang Freddie Mercury, and he was exactly right. If friends can't help us in difficult times, then what are friends for?

Some "friends" are particularly important for you in getting the word out about your organization—the ones who can be multipliers for your efforts. These might be any non-profit or business organization that aligns with your organization's goals or might benefit from a joint effort.

For example, various chambers of commerce, trade associations, and local business clubs can serve as multipliers for your non-profit. Make sure that you sign up for their event list, select popular events, attend, and use your networking skills to find some great contacts who would be excited about your non-profit.

I always follow a win-win approach, offering partnering organizations access to resources or connections that might help them in reaching their goals.

For example, if you know of a service or product produced by a small business in your area which may help your stakeholders or clients resolve their needs or challenges, connect them with your circle. Make sure that you include their offering in your brochure or newsletters. After all, if your newly-built connection benefits from interaction with you, the next step will be an unexpected referral to a potential donor or funder for your organization.

Finally, don't forget to visit your local Chamber of Commerce and meet with its management team. Find out about the latest events and volunteer to help with the organization. This will not go unnoticed, and there's a healthy chance that at the very event you helped to organize, there will be that one "lucky" encounter where you will achieve your goals in a single handshake.

Exercise:

Get a list of upcoming events at your local chamber of commerce and start networking with purpose. Make it a point to introduce your organization to at least three promising leads. Which event are you attending this week?

_____

_____

_____

_____

_____

_____

Networking Online with LinkedIn

With all this old-fashioned shoe-leather, let's not entirely forget the technology tools that are at our fingertips. One of the most powerful and often-neglected tools is LinkedIn, the world's largest professional network. With LinkedIn, you can reach people in a personal way and build relationships that translate into actual funds for your organization. Here is how you can dramatically increase your outreach to new leads and prospects, so you can make that fantastic leap forward just before your Board begins to wonder—where is that new development director?

If you think that LinkedIn is just a recruiters' paradise, think twice. Today LinkedIn is the de-facto leader among the professional social media platforms. Every second, a new customer signs up to LinkedIn to be a part of the robust 500 million+ network of professionals all over the world. That's one great database you can put to a great use! Interestingly, according to the most recent (January 2019) statistics from LinkedIn, of all the LinkedIn users, only half use LinkedIn on a monthly basis, and only 3 million share content on a weekly basis—just a touch over 1% of monthly users. This equals to 3 million users getting 9 billion impressions each week! Are you with me? If you want to be successful, you need to be one of those active users!

However, in order to hit the mark on LinkedIn, you need to know some navigation rules. In my fundraising experience, the best results have been achieved by those organizations which developed a solid organization's page that was always up-to-date. I also recommend signing up for LinkedIn's paid service. This service provides you with InMail, a laser-sharp tool that can tear down the walls of mistrust and bring easy victories. The InMail service offers you the chance to approach any LinkedIn subscriber with no prior connection to you. Just imagine—you can get past the toughest gatekeepers in the world! In my own practice, I was able to connect with funders and build an entire partnership network in a different country by using InMail alone. Moreover, simple but targeted messages through InMail helped me to raise funds and nurture new relationships.

How?

Very simple—just find some time in your schedule today and follow the steps below:

1. Do LinkedIn research on key funders in the area you're interested in.

2. Select ten solid leads and take time to learn about their professional backgrounds and affiliations.

3. Make sure that you take serious note of any existing connections between these target individuals and your connections.

4. Once you feel comfortable with each candidate, draft a short message.

5. Do not forget to include your core request in the first paragraph, i.e. "I'm contacting you to share a new community development project focused on _____(area of interest of your target organization) "

6. Follow up with another email—or better yet—a phone call after four days.

7. If possible, invite your counterpart to an off-line meeting at a local coffee shop or offer to host him or her at your office to discuss possible collaboration.

Exercise:

Follow the above seven steps for at least five leads, and track your progress below.

Lead #1:_____

Lead #2:_____

Lead #3:_____

Lead #4:_____

Lead#5:_____

A Letter from Russell Wilson: Should You Work with Celebrities?

Okay, here's the last word on expanding your network. I said at the beginning, "think big," right? So, should you go for celebrity support or not waste your time?

I know that the world is divided into those who love Tom Brady, and those who can't stand him. For me, I don't really care, as I was brought up on soccer and love Messi!

Yet, as far as my two sons are concerned, we have a rivalry going between Aaron Rodgers and Russell Wilson.

Here is the story on how one of them actually connected with our family. One day I told my son, "Why don't you write a message to your favorite sports star?"

Victor is really into the Seahawks, and dreams that they will repeat their 2014 Super Bowl success. Russell Wilson, the Seahawks quarterback, has been his role model for a while.

So, here is what Victor wrote to him:

Dear Russell,

My name is Victor and I'm 9 years old. I really like watching you play, and would love it if you sent me your autograph. I love the Seahawks, and whenever you play, I'm always excited.

Thank you so much,
Victor

Granted, I used a database of top celebrity contact info (more on this below) to get his address, and all we did was to put it in an envelope and mail it to Russell. Frankly, I had my doubts. But I also thought, *Why don't we give it a try?*

A few months later, the day before Victor's birthday, an envelope arrived, stamped in Seattle, WA. The envelope contained the simple letter with a signature that said:

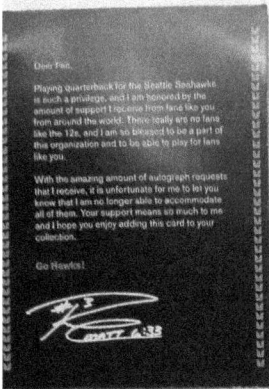

FRONTLINE
ATHLETE MANAGEMENT

April 17, 2017

Dear Fan,

Thank you for taking the time to write a letter to Russell Wilson. He asked me to send you the enclosed autographed football card and to thank you for watching his games.

Go Hawks!

Susan Schmidt

Enclosure

frontlineathletes.com

The reason for my telling you this is not to convince you to write to your favorite Hollywood or sports star (even though you may want to try that as well just for fun), but rather use this as an encouragement for you to reach out to top people who may support your non-profit and social cause that you are so passionately trying to advance.

As David Schwab, VP of Octagon, a global sports and entertainment company, suggests in Forbes, "As a non-profit marketer, don't ever discard the possibility of working with influencers to promote your cause. Instead, consider it a potential game changer for your organization. With astute planning, you can attract talent that will work for your cause to create effective messaging and maximize awareness."[11]

Schwab also recommends being selective in terms of celebrity outreach, only choosing those who genuinely care for your cause, and have had some similar engagements in the past. Most importantly, he cautions non-profits from going into a monetary relationship in the wrong direction—that is, never pay a

---

[11] https://www.forbes.com/sites/davidschwab/2016/06/02/the-nuances-of-celebrity-and-non-profit-collaboration/#7a93a1cb2a73

celebrity to endorse your cause. An endorsement can be a big boost but needs to come naturally.

Here is what you can do now to reach out to these people:

- Research which celebrities have an affinity for your cause.
- Get a database of the stars and find the address and contacts for these influencers. For example, you can test out a seven-day trial for Contact Any Celebrity.[12]
- Write a short letter explaining how your cause may benefit this influencer.
- Send it over.

You may be surprised at what is going to happen next!

*A Word of Caution: We are all human. Humans make mistakes. Yet, when your chosen celebrity makes a mistake or even worse—falls into criminal behavior (think Jared Fogle of Subway fame, or Bill Cosby, etc.)—it may become a disaster for your non-profit. As David

---

[12] https://contactanycelebrity.com/cac

Vinjamuri, the Forbes magazine contributor noted, "Beyond the risk that the celebrity will behave badly, there are other potential issues for the brand. The most important is the possibility that the celebrity will distract the brand . . . When you get a celebrity to endorse your brand, you're trying to co-opt their brand expertise, and their fans to your brand. And there's no guarantee that they'll match, or even imprint."[13]

---

[13]https://www.forbes.com/sites/davidvinjamuri/2015/08/19/will
-jared-kill-subway-the-perils-of-celebrity-
endorsement/#475445b5448b

Dr. Andrey N. Gidaspov

Part 2: Share and Act

The Power of the Ask

I can never find a better quote than the one from the legendary Hank Rosso, who said, "Fundraising is the gentle art of teaching the joy of giving."

Think about this: The joy of giving. That's all.

Yet that joy will never come to fruition unless you take a very important step—make the ask.

Just like dating, everyone knows there's an inevitable request coming . . . it's just a matter of timing. It's natural to be nervous.

"Hi, my name is Jane... And I'm an asker... Can I ask you for a favor ?!"

I recently stopped at a busy intersection and saw someone asking for help. It was a middle-aged man wearing shoddy clothes with a desperate look on his face. He was holding a sign "Please Help Me! I Lost My Home!" Yet he didn't look at any of the drivers; he just stared off somewhere beyond the busy traffic. The sign said it all. Or so he hoped.

But nobody cared. A young woman in a little blue Toyota Prius on the right side was busy talking on her cellphone. A truck driver enjoyed loud country music.

I sensed that the homeless man really needed help. Even though I didn't have much, I thought I could spare some change I had left for the toll road. I pulled down my window and waved to the guy. He didn't show any signs of seeing me. I was in the farthest lane from him, and the light was about to change.

Last try—but the guy still didn't look. Alas, he didn't get anything from this bunch of cars. The light changed, and I had to go.

Just holding the sign is not enough, especially in our busy lives. It's sad, but it happens everywhere. Worthy causes, great non-profits, urgent needs are not covered just because there is one missing component.

As Deb Mills-Scofield, a strategy and innovation consultant at Glengary LLC, suggests in HBR, "When we don't use the power of the ask, we are in essence saying 'no' before the question has even been asked—saying no to opportunities that change our businesses, our organizations, ourselves . . . and actual lives. So even if it feels uncomfortable, look for even just a small way you can use the power of the ask in your network—for someone you work for, with, or manage."

"Learn to ask for what you want," says Dr. Thomas T. Hills, a professor of psychology at University of Warwick. Dr. Hills cited a study by researchers at UC Santa Cruz in which a female student was asked to pose as a panhandler asking people on the street for money. The interesting thing was that when the student employed "the 'just ask' condition," 22% of people offered money, with an average gift of about 50 cents. However, if the student was more specific requesting an odd amount of money like 17 cents, the results were even more impressive, with 36% people throwing coins into the hat.[14] So ask often and ask for your specific project in an engaging way. You'll get more.

---

[14] https://www.psychologytoday.com/us/blog/statistical-life/201402/if-you-want-more-out-life-just-ask

Learn to Ask: How a Street Artist Ended Up with Over $1.2M

Have you heard the story of Amanda Palmer? [15] Amanda worked as a street artist, a statue with a painted face, standing in front of crowds to get donations in her hat. She says that she loved the moment of intensive eye contact with strangers, which she says people are lacking these days. She had the ask in her eyes. Since then, Amanda has perfected her ask for her band when she's on the road. Very often Amanda uses the moments after the gig to ask for help, when she's trying to spread the word about her free online music.

Unexpectedly, when she simply asks, people hand over dollar bills. So, finally, she decided to use crowdfunding to help her band. And the unexpected happened. While she was trying to raise just $100,000, over 24,000 people contributed to support her band which led to an astonishing $1.2 million raised online!

"How did you make them do it?" exclaimed media critics.

---

[15] https://www.ted.com/talks/amanda_palmer_the_art_of_asking

"I didn't make them do it, I just asked them," says Amanda. "Through this very act of asking people, I connected with them."

The ask is essential in fundraising!

And what's in it for the giver? No less than happiness, affirms Arthur Brooks, President of American Enterprise Institute. As Brooks describes in his article,[16] he encountered an interesting pattern in the data while working on his book on charitable giving. Brooks realized that donors benefited from their benevolence not only morally, but monetarily as well. Their income grew after they made their gifts! According to Harvard and the University of British Columbia research, "Charitable giving improves what psychologists call "self-efficacy," one's belief that one is capable of handling a situation and bringing about a desired outcome. When people give their time or money to a cause they believe in, they become problem solvers. Problem solvers are happier than bystanders and victims of circumstance."

---

[16] Ibid

Preparing for Your Ask: Learning About Your Donor and Mastering Your Pitch

So how do we ask effectively?

First, you need to define how much you should ask for from each potential donor. Joan Garry, a fundraising consultant, always likes "to shoot for more." As she notes in her blog,[17] she usually uses what she calls her "white horse" strategy. "You, Mr. Donor, have the opportunity, thanks to your good fortune, to make a lead gift that could move our work from four cities to eight. That could allow us to move now so we don't miss a full academic year."

To accomplish a successful ask, however, Garry suggests that you need to be well prepared. Learn everything you can about the donor and his or her past interaction with your or similar non-profits. Most importantly, "regardless of whether you are asking someone for $1,000 or $250,000, you need a clear, compelling pitch. It needs to be inspirational, credible, and tangible, and you have to include a goosebump moment."

---

[17] http://www.joangarry.com/how-to-ask-for-donations/

Your ask should always connect the dots and include a specific amount. One Street,[18] an international non-profit organization, provides the following example of the direct ask[19]: "Well, I think we've found some exciting connections here today. It looks like our organization is addressing many of your needs through our current Safe Routes to Schools program. Could you contribute $5,000 to help us meet our goal this year of adding another school to the program?"

Marc Pitman, a successful fundraiser and fundraising coach, believes that the two most useful asks are:[20]

1. "Would you consider a gift of $X?" This is a down-to-earth, concrete approach that helps you and the donor resolve the matter swiftly.
2. "Honestly, I have NO idea how much to ask you for, but is a gift of $_____ something you'd be able to consider?"

---

[18] http://www.onestreet.org/who-we-are
[19] http://www.onestreet.org/management/64-hiddenstuff/hiddenstuff/120-fundraising-tips-the-direct-ask
[20] http://fundraisingcoach.com/2012/05/08/2-phrases-to-use-when-asking-for-money/

"This is a request for help," explains Pitman, "an honest way to show your willingness to hear the donor. It also helps volunteers who want to ask for a higher level than they are comfortable with."

Is that it? Not yet. In the final moment, you need to use one of the most important tools of fundraising: silence.

"He who speaks next, loses," notes Gail Perry, one of the most effective fundraising consultants in the U.S. Like many other star fundraisers, Gail advises that you must leave the space to the donor after you've made your ask.[21] This is a sacred moment of silence. Let the donor weigh options and give you an answer.

Also, beware of the ten common errors when asking for a gift,[22] warns Kristin Clarke, ASAE & The Center for Association Leadership. The donors can sense your lack of preparation and fear of the ask, and that might turn them away. However, if you don't ask for a specific amount or "talk too much and don't listen," you will likely to hear a two-letter response.

---

[21] http://www.gailperry.com/2013/10/six-steps-perfect-ask/
[22] http://www.asaecenter.org/Resources/whitepaperdetail.cf m?ItemNumber=32284

Exercise:

How often are you making specific "asks" for your non-profit?

_____

_____

Which steps outlined above have you used? What worked, and what didn't?

_____

_____

Consider an upcoming opportunity to ask. Script your ideal conversation. Practice this with someone you trust.

Always Be Looking

I used to say, "Always be asking," but people thought I meant that you need to be like that ubiquitous used car salesman. No! No! No! Instead, always be looking. You need to look for opportunities, listen, and observe and understand people around you, be they donors, partners, or supporters.

We've talked about it already—99% of people do not want to ask for money. Yet, if you are serious about your non-profit, and if you don't want to waste weeks and months of important work for your valuable cause, you need to seriously commit to be asking each and every time you have a solid opportunity to do so.

The key is to practice your elevator pitch and then customize it for different scenarios.

Are you with me?

Basically, there are so many non-profits that are losing huge amounts of contributions by simply missing opportunities.

I was at a meeting with our executive team trying to convince a long-standing supporter and donor to commit to a major gift. Yet, despite their eloquent presentation on the organization's achievements and huge importance of committing the funds for this new effort, the donor was not moved. He simply wasn't very responsive. In fact, he was rushing to another meeting, and apologized that he had to go.

I motioned to help him out.

On the way back to the car, which was a three-minute walk, I thought that I sensed a lightness, an openness in him. I thought, I'll make a leap of faith and just ask.

I simply asked the donor whether he was interested in establishing his legacy with us, indicating that the lead gift was well within his means. It turned out that he wasn't aware of the lead-gift amount, and he stopped to think about it. I saw some hope there. I kept silent. He said that he would discuss it with his spouse and get back to me. And that was that.

Little did I know that when I returned home, I would get a phone call back from the donor's spouse who happily informed me that they'd decided to make the lead gift!

I am not here to brag about these experiences, but to reiterate that it is important to always be ready to ask!

Dr. Andrey N. Gidaspov

Exercise:

In order to make sure you're always, always ready, you need to get your elevator pitch down solid. Take these steps soon:

1. Review your elevator pitch (see the chapter on "Networking with Purpose" for specific pointers).
2. If you've been using your pitch for a while now, think about how you might tweak it to share the impact of your non-profit with an emotional story.
3. Keep practicing it, so that it's smooth and natural.
4. Use it every single time that you feel there is an opportunity to impress your prospect.

Direct Mail—Really?

I know there are some who are skeptical about this heading. Who loves mail? But what if it's from an organization you care about?

I put on my sneakers, open the door and walk out into the drizzle. It usually takes me thirty-four steps to get to my mailbox. I lean against a huge oak tree, and a bunch of cold acorns land right on my head. Ouch!

I pull out a little metal key from my pocket, and reach into the mailbox. No news there—I'm walking back with a whole bunch of junk mail, knowing what exactly is going to the recycling bin straight away.

As I head back into the house, I recall that the Direct Mail Association (DMA) Factbook published the results of its recent research, stating that this year 65% of consumers of all ages purchased a product advertised by direct mail. Furthermore, based on a 2018 DMA Response Rate Report, direct mail response rates reached 9% and 5% for house and prospect lists respectively. Compare these rates to 3.6% and 1.6% for the same in 2003-2015! Even better, email had only 1% response rate for both lists![23]

Isn't it amazing?

My junk mail pile is now on the kitchen table. Temporarily. I can almost feel how each envelope is trying to impress me.

But I am not. In fact, I am on automatic pilot.

There are two piles, one is very small; another one is a mountain-high.

Let's see, Macy's new catalog—zip, gone. New distance education courses? Hmm, not this time. Another credit-card offer? You must be kidding me, Cardinal Bank. And so most of it goes into the mountainous pile on my table.

Aha, finally, here is some personal mail I want to keep. This is real mail.

But wait a minute, two envelopes grab my attention. On the first one I see a little child suffering from famine. Her eyes are desperate. She needs help. And the message is clear. Nineteen dollars will give a rabbit to this girl in an African village. Thirty-five dollars will provide five little ducks. Seventy-five dollars will bring a nice goat. Everything's clear. I am interested.

---

[23] https://www.iwco.com/blog/2019/01/16/direct-mail-response-rates-dominate-other-channels/

Another one also piqued my curiosity. It is a very unique, brown-colored envelope with a picture of a moose and forest on the background. I tear it open and see a long letter on fancy paper. The letter suggests that I need to look into hunting. If I become a member, I get a couple of razor-sharp knives for free and discounts on rifles. Seriously?

Do these people know that I'm not even remotely interested in hunting? They probably purchased the list from the *Western Horseman* magazine I got for free with my miles, or something like that.

All these nicely-printed letters and offers of cheap rifles fly like rockets into the garbage. So, does direct mail actually work? Yes, if done right.

At one of the non-profits that I worked with, there were several staff members with a "been there, done that" attitude. Unfortunately, they worked for the development department.

When I looked at the results of their donor communication, I noticed that the mailing was quite sparse. It was only done once or twice max, at the end of the year.

When I asked them, "Why don't you try to do it more often," the answer was: "No, we shouldn't spam them! And in fact, there was a consultant who tried to do that in the past, and it just didn't work out."

I wasn't surprised because this is a common mistake for many non-profits. The notion that somehow the donors and prospects will be tired of your "spam" messages is widespread.

Of course, if your intention is to send annoying, uninformative, dull, and boring messages, then it will become a self-fulfilling prophecy.

However, if you want to have more contributions at the end of your year, and most importantly, want to deepen your relationships with your existing donors, then invest time and effort in creating multiple "touch points" with your donor base. Also, learn how to say "thank you" more often, via your newsletter, email or a personal call. Once I increased the volume of communication with the donors of that non-profit, the results were stunning. We doubled our annual giving levels, and also developed much more intimate connections with our donors and partners.

Here are my guidelines for making direct mail work:

1. You have to know your customers. Don't waste your money trying to buy generic lists. Your letters will end up in the trash almost immediately. Talk to experienced consultants specializing in direct mail response. Find out

which database will be best for your industry sector. If you can, start with your own list.

2. Your letter should grab people's attention, so that your client opens it. The next step, of course, is to make sure that you have a clear message and unique supporting graphics.

3. You need to test various options. Test, test, test. Mark your mail with QR codes or simple numbers to make sure to re-use your winning copy for other campaigns.

Joe Garecht, an experienced fundraising professional and owner of The Fundraising Authority website, suggests designing letters targeted to three types of recipients: "the 10 second club, the skimmers, and the readers." Joe notes that while the first group will throw your mail to the trash in 10 seconds, the second group will hold it for about half a minute, while the readers will hold it for an eternity—1-2 minutes! The key is to attract your reader by using the best focus areas like the first line, and the P.S. To capitalize on this, make sure that you bold, italicize, and use captions. The final part is easy; ask a concrete amount for a measurable service.

Exercise:

1. Take out your organization's most recent direct mailing. Analyze its language. Does it make sense from the customer's perspective? Does it follow the proven pattern for successful direct mail language ... or is it TOO creative?

2. Practice collecting the best pieces of direct mail that you receive at home—the ones that actually move you to donate. Keep these in a "swipe file" that you can always use for your own mailing.

Part 3: Treasure Your Donors

HARNESS THE POWER OF CONNECTION

One of your top priorities as a fundraiser is to keep your donors happy. In fact, every donor on whatever level he or she has given, should be celebrated and treasured as long as your non-profit lives! It may sound like hyperbole, but donors literally are your gold, and you need to treasure your wealth. The section includes a few simple ways to do so.

What is Donor Stewardship?

Donor stewardship basically means that your relationship with the donor should not end with one thank you note (which is a great beginning!) and newsletter subscription. Rather, donor stewardship is the constantly-evolving process of deepening your interactive engagement with your donor for years to come.

As Joe Garecht suggests, [24] donor stewardship, done the right way, will help your donors give more and give often. It will transform them in such a way that they

---

[24] http://www.thefundraisingauthority.com/donor-cultivation/3-goals-donor-stewardship/

will upgrade their giving levels. And importantly, they will also keep referring new prospects along the way.

Let's look at some statistics.

The AFP and Urban Institute surveyed 3,000 non-profits in 2012 and found that for "every 100 donors that were acquired, about 107 were lost."[25]

MarketSmart developed a unique Fundraising Report Card[26] tool, which analyzes data from 4,200+ organizations. For donors giving at under a $100 level in February, 2018, their donor retention rate was just 20.45%. This means that overall only 20% of donors at this level would renew their donation in 2019!

That's an alarming number! Why are we losing donors so liberally? Is there a special trick that can keep those donors loyal to your organization?

It turns out there are no tricks. Instead, it's quite simple—you have to thank and listen, then thank and listen to your donors. If you will do just that, you will be absolutely fine.

Here is my list of the top 7 things you must do to have a warm relationship with your donors:

---

[25] https://www.classy.org/blog/donor-stewardship-how-to-stop-losing-your-donors/

[26] https://fundraisingreportcard.com/

1. Thank your donor immediately after you've received the gift (within 24-48 hours).
2. Thank the donor again with regularly scheduled phone calls throughout the year (I recommend one per quarter).
3. Keep them abreast of news about your organization.
4. Invite them to meaningful events that your non-profit or your partners hold.
5. Give them a small token of appreciation.
6. Celebrate their giving.
7. Be their genuine friend (in real terms!).

Back in 2011, over 250 non-profit organizations worked with DonorVoice to provide their ways of keeping their donors loyal and satisfied. According to that survey,[27] donors indicated the following values that were extremely important to them:

- Donor perceives organization to be effective.
- Donor knows what to expect with each interaction.
- Donor receives a timely thank you.

---

[27] http://www.thedonorvoice.com/wp-content/uploads/downloads/2011/09/DonorVoice_Donor-Commitment-Study_2011-Executive-Summary_final2.pdf

- Donor receives opportunities to make views known.
- Donor feels like he or she is a part of an important cause.
- Donor feels his or her involvement is appreciated.
- Donor receives information showing who is being helped.[28]

---

[28] https://bloomerang.co/retention

The Power of a Hand-Written Letter

"I wake filled with thoughts of you. Your portrait and the intoxicating evening which we spent yesterday have left my senses in turmoil . . . what a strange effect you have on my heart! Yielding to the profound feelings which overwhelm me, I draw from your lips, from your heart a love which consumes me with fire? Until then, mio dolce amor, a thousand kisses; but give me none in return, for they set my blood on fire."

A powerful romantic letter, isn't it? Can you guess who the author is? Well, let's leave it for the end of this chapter. While I never received a letter like the above, I did once receive the following message from an astonished prospective donor:

"Dear Andrey,

It's been a while since I received a sincere letter, and even longer since I got a hand-written note. Thank you so much for your enthusiasm in describing your non-profit project. I will most definitely get back in touch with you next time I'll be in Washington. Let's get in touch in a month or so. My cell is ...Talk to you soon, X"

We had just met, and trust me, I didn't pen any passionate prose. I'd just acknowledged the pleasure of meeting a new person in my life. I was respectful of someone else's time and insights.

Dr. Christopher Peterson shares that "a good letter is personal and personalized. A good letter takes time to write. The thing about writing a letter is that no one can multitask while doing so, unlike e-mails or telephone calls. A letter represents undivided attention and is precious as a consequence. Oh, yes, a good letter is handwritten, not a cut-and-pasted, global searched-and-replaced bit of faux intimacy."[29]

In our deeply isolationist digital time, any act of showing your true human side is worth gold. It is that splash that works on an emotional level. It is never manipulation, and always a sincere gesture of appreciation. Try it the next time you meet your new prospect, returning customer, or colleague.

And yes, the letter in the beginning. It was written by one of the best military geniuses and strategists the

---

[29] https://www.psychologytoday.com/us/blog/the-good-life/200912/does-anyone-write-letters-anymore

world has known—Napoleon Bonaparte. He wrote it to his true love, Josephine. Should we learn from Napoleon?

Exercise:

1. Go to a nice stationery store and take your time. Get a stock of stationary. Select a card that you feel is the most appropriate for the moment.
2. Clear your desk. Make sure that you have your card, envelope, and a blue ink pen.
3. Think.
4. Write like you're writing to your best friend.
5. Sign.
6. Seal the envelope.
7. Send on the same day.

You'll see results soon.

Dr. Andrey N. Gidaspov

Nothing Can Beat the Power of Listening

As a fundraiser, if you need to own any superpowers, listening is top on the list. Again, and again, I've experienced it during my non-profit work. At times, the donor subtly mentions something so important, that unless you listen carefully, you might miss it—and it may never come up in conversation again.

One day, I was sitting with a donor in his eighties, who shared with me his whole family story and his profound experience with illness. Only after that did he mention that he was considering giving a legacy gift. However, he said he really wanted to see a little token of appreciation from the organization, like a fancy pin. None of us thought the pin would be of any interest to anyone these days, but that donor really wanted it! So, of course we did it.

How can you listen to your donors better?

"Call me, will you, please?"

That's literally what an elderly donor said to me one day. No one from the organization had ever called him on the phone!

I admit, in the texting and VR world of today, it's not so trendy to use the phone. But, if you truly want to reach folks in your donor base, you MUST call them. Have a plan, and make calls every single day. This rapidly vanishing skill of two or more humans speaking to each other is essential to any fundraiser, whether she's twenty or fifty or eighty years old. If you develop this discipline of active calling and thanking donors, you will quickly see results.

I refuse to believe that a simple phone call to a current donor may be a challenging task. Having done many cold calls in my career, I'm so happy when I'm able to call an existing customer just to ask him, "How have you been, Old Sport?"

You can make your phone call more effective if you:

- Learn as much as you can about your counterpart's donation history.
- Thank the donor for his continuous support of the organization.
- Surprise the donor with some exciting initiative that only she can help advance.
- Make sure that you leave room for other ideas and projects that the donor might be interested in supporting.
- In case the donor surprises you with a sudden urge to give, be ready with handy information about the easiest way to donate for the project.

Exercise:

1. Make a list of donors you treasure the most. Commit to calling each of them this week.

2. Go through your donation records with your team, and schedule phone calls with all your donors. You should make at least five calls per day, and hold yourself to your schedule!

Join Me in My Life-Long Learning Journey

Like any trade, fundraising is a life-long learning process, and I'm still on my journey.

I don't know where you are in your journey, but wherever you are, I hope that you've found a gem or two in this book. I recommend that you pick a few of the approaches and think about how they might work for you. If you don't try, you may miss some golden opportunities right in your own backyard.

However, I also recommend that you read as many other fundraising books as possible, seek out resources, attend conferences, and take part in webinars and workshops. You never know when you'll see a great idea or method that you can implement right away. I do it all the time. Below is my list of suggested reading for you. These are the authors I trust, and I've certainly used their advice in my practice.

I invite you to send me a line or two with your thoughts about the book, or any of the methods that I've recommended. My email is andrey@gidaspov.com.

You may also want to subscribe to FundrzrTV, my YouTube channel, where I have weekly postings on fundraising tips and much more.

Finally, if you are a small non-profit and have limited resources to invest in your development, please join my 100 Non-Profits Initiative. With this initiative, I can showcase your non-profit on my YouTube Channel and my site, get you more visibility and hopefully more funding opportunities along the way.

Thanks, and enjoy your journey!

Recommended Reading:

1. *The Fundraiser's Guide to Irresistible Communications* by Jeff Brooks
2. *The Generosity Network: New Transformational Tools for Successful Fund-Raising* by Jennifer McCrea
3. *The Little Book of Gold: Fundraising for Small (and Very Small) Nonprofits* by Erik Hanberg
4. *Asking: A 59-Minute Guide to Everything Board Members, Volunteers, and Staff Must Know to Secure the Gift, Newly Revised Edition* by Jerold Panas
5. *Effective Fundraising for Nonprofits: Real-World Strategies That Work* by Ilona Bray
6. *How to Write Fundraising Materials That Raise More Money: The Art, the Science, the Secrets* by Tom Ahern
7. *Yours for the Asking: An Indispensable Guide to Fundraising and Management* by Reynold Levy
8. *Engagement Fundraising: How to raise more money for less in the 21st century* by Greg Warner
9. *Mega Gifts: 2nd Edition, Revised & Updated* by Jerold Panas

10. *The Digital Fundraising Blueprint: How to Raise More Money Online for Your Nonprofit* by Jeremy Haselwood

11. *The Eight Principles of Sustainable Fundraising: Transforming Fundraising Anxiety into the Opportunity of a Lifetime* by Larry Johnson

About the Author
Andrey N. Gidaspov, Ph.D.

Andrey Gidaspov has over twenty-five years of experience in international business development, strategic partnership building, global fundraising, and non-profit management. For the past ten years, Andrey has led numerous successful strategic development and fundraising initiatives for large mission-driven non-profits in the U.S. and internationally. His areas of fundraising expertise are individual giving, corporate outreach, and crowdfunding campaigns. His belief in the power of personal relationships and creative social media outreach are key components of his success. Earlier in his career, Andrey managed his own boutique consulting business in Hong Kong, developing successful solutions for multiple U.S. and international clients in IT outsourcing, mobile application, and mobile content development areas in China, Japan, and Southeast Asia. His experience also includes ten years at the US Department of Commerce, where he helped hundreds of U.S. small and medium technology businesses to find reliable partners in Eurasia. Andrey has lived and worked in six countries and speaks Chinese and Russian. Andrey and his family currently reside in Northern Virginia.